NATIONAL GEOGRAPHIC

Ladders

Speak Out

Getting the W

by Barbara Keeler

Communication in Early Civilization

Nobody knows when humans began to **communicate,** but it may have been about 5,400 years ago. Their first messages might have been in the form of cave art.

Primitive people used different ways to communicate across short distances. Smoke signals went as far as the eye could see, and drums sounded as far as the ear could hear.

People probably spoke long before they wrote. Without writing, it was hard to preserve messages and send them long distances. An oral message passed through generations was only as accurate as the memory of the human telling it. Even today, some languages have no written form.

After early people invented writing, ideas could be preserved, copied, and sent to people in other places. Communication could be **transmitted** with accuracy over time and between locations.

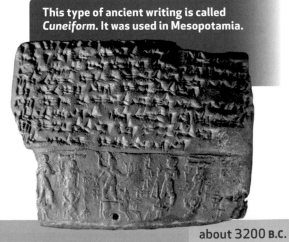

This type of ancient writing is called *Cuneiform*. It was used in Mesopotamia.

These cave paintings in Lascaux, France are about 17,000 years old.

15,000 B.C.

5000 B.C.

about 3200 B.C.
earliest writing in Mesopotamia

around 15,000 B.C.
earliest known cave paintings at Lascaux, France

between 3400 and 3200 B.C.
earliest known Egyptian writing

At first, written messages were carved into hard surfaces. Then the Egyptians invented paper-like sheets using the papyrus plant. With lighter-weight writing material, messages could be easily carried over a distance.

Egyptians began to use a postal service around 2000 B.C. About 600 B.C., Persians used a system of mounted messengers. Horseback riders worked in relay, stopping regularly to change horses or pass their messages to another rider.

Pigeons could also carry lighter messages. Mesopotamians used carrier pigeons as early as 2500 B.C.

Egyptians made the paper-like papyrus from leaves of the papyrus plant.

This ancient Mayan text was written between 300 and 200 B.C.

about 3000 B.C.
Egyptians use papyrus sheets for writing

about 2000 B.C.
postal service in Egypt

2500 B.C.

0

2500 B.C.
carrier pigeons carry messages in Mesopotamia

400–300 B.C.
earliest known writing in Central America

105 B.C.
paper invented in China

Printing Spreads the Word

After years of rolling papyrus into scrolls, people began binding pages into books. Books were easier to store and move than scrolls.

However, each page of a book had to be handwritten. If someone wanted a copy of a book, it could take years to copy it. Therefore, few books were available, and most people did not learn to read.

In 1455, Johannes Gutenberg invented a printing press. Unlike earlier printing blocks, it had movable letters, which could form an unlimited amount of words. In less time than it had taken to hand copy one book, printers could publish thousands of books.

This Chinese typesetting plate revolves making it easier for printers to use.

1455
printing
press invented

100

1300

1400

Chinese printing
blocks invented

1295
Marco Polo returned to Italy from China and brought
along the understanding of block-letter printing.
Italians began to use block letters for printing.

As a result, more people had access to information. And so books became the primary learning tool, and more people learned to read.

Printing current news and events also became possible. The first daily newspaper was published in 1650. Later when the typewriter was invented, people could type messages faster than they could write them. According to many historians, Mark Twain was the first author to submit a typewritten book manuscript in 1883.

Gutenberg adapted an olive oil press to create his printing press. He used metal blocks. They were long lasting and easy to move.

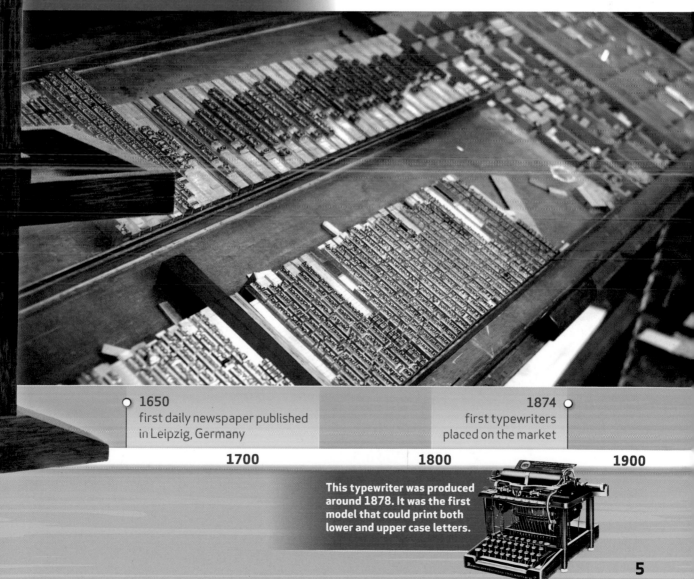

1650 first daily newspaper published in Leipzig, Germany	1874 first typewriters placed on the market
1700	1800	1900

This typewriter was produced around 1878. It was the first model that could print both lower and upper case letters.

Early Telecommunications

Spreading messages was still slow and difficult even after printing was invented. Oral or written, messages could only travel by person, animal, or boat. For example, the Declaration of Independence was printed in early July of 1776, but it did not reach England until August 10, 1776.

In the 1830s, inventors used a telegraph to transmit messages over wires using signals called *Morse code*. A person receiving the signals translated them into words on a paper document called a telegram. Messages could be sent across the country. Wires soon connected all major United States cities, and cables were laid under the Atlantic Ocean. Newspapers could publish news from across the world on the day events happened.

Model of the first electric telegraph

Joseph Henry

Morse code uses short and long pulses to represent letters and numbers. Sounds, lights, or written dots and dashes are all used for communicating Morse code. A "dot" is a short pulse. A "dash" is a long pulse.

● ● ●   ▬ ▬ ▬   ● ● ●
● **S**   **O**   **S**

1832
Joseph Henry invents the first electric telegraph.

1835
Samuel Morse and Alfred Vail invent Morse code.

1800   **1820**   **1840**

1844 ○
The first long-distance electric telegraph line is constructed between Baltimore, MD and Washington, DC.

Later that century, another invention made it possible to speak to someone miles away. In 1876, crowds gathered at a telegraph office and sang into a telephone receiver. In another office six miles away, the inventor of the telephone, Alexander Graham Bell, listened.

By 1880, about 30,000 telephones were in use in the United States. By 1915, telephone lines stretched from coast to coast.

Tele-Everything

The names for the new communication devices weren't just clever word play. The inventors used Greek and Latin word parts to name their new devices.

Tele- means *distant* or *over a distance;* *-gram* means *writing* or *recording;* *phone* comes from *phon* or *phono* and means *sound, voice,* or *speech.*

The first phones used a single hole for speaking and listening. To call another phone, a person stuck a finger into the hole and scratched a metal plate. If the other person heard the scratching on the other phone, he or she would respond.

1860

1880

1900

1876
first telephone call

1892
Alexander Graham Bell makes first cross-country call from New York to Chicago.

Up to the Minute Communications

The telegraph and telephone could send messages between places connected by wires. But they were not helpful for a ship at sea. During the 1900s, however, scientists learned to send messages without wires through the air. In 1901, wireless telegraph messages were sent across the Atlantic Ocean. In 1906, vocal transmission allowed two people to talk to each other on wireless radios, even if they were on ships. The advancement of sending wireless messages laid the foundation to develop portable wireless phones.

At first, radios were used for two-way conversations. After a station sent one-way radio **broadcasts** to larger audiences, people bought radios for their homes. Later cars came with radios installed. Radios became a major source of news. Events could be reported within the same hour they happened. People also relied on radio broadcasts for music and entertainment.

Later models of radios were small enough to be set on tabletops. Just like today, finding ways to reduce the size of pieces of technology was an example of technological progress.

Early radios were built like cabinets and stood in corners of homes like pieces of furniture.

first commercial radio station launched

1900   **1910**   **1920**

1906
first experimental
radio broadcast

1921
first World Series
baseball game
broadcast via radio

When television was invented, moving pictures could be broadcast as well as sound. People were amazed by the television set that was unveiled at the 1939 World's Fair. Even so, the use of radio was much more widespread.

Over the next decade, as television became more popular, it also gained the power to influence. Television commercials, news, and entertainment began to shape people's opinions and attitudes.

1930   1940   1950

1939
first television demonstrated at the New York World's Fair

In the early 1940s, TVs became smaller and no longer took up space in homes like large pieces of furniture.

The Computer Age

Computers revolutionized communication again. Researchers developed computers during World War II. Many government agencies were using computers by the late 1960s. People could do their work faster and store it in the computer. Even so, people could still not access and share written information as easily as they wanted. For that, they turned to published books, newspapers, or magazines. If they did not own the resource, they had to go to a library. That is, until the Internet was available.

The first computers were enormous and costly.

1946
first general-purpose,
all-electronic computer

1971
electronic mail, or
e-mail, invented

1950

1960

1970

1960
first video
game created:
SpaceWar!

1969
early form of the
Internet created

During the 1960s, researchers developed a system for computers to share information over wires. In 1969, they created an early form of the Internet. And computers at government agencies and universities began sharing data. By 1971, engineers had created electronic mail, or e-mail. Later computers could share data without wires. A vision of laptop computers was also taking shape. The DynaBook was an idea for a laptop meant for children, but it was never produced. In the early 1980s, the first laptops were produced and sold.

In the 1990s, a world-wide **network** of computers developed for data sharing launched the *World Wide Web*. Web service providers connected millions of businesses and homes to each other.

The personal computer and the Internet transformed the world. People could get more information more quickly than ever before. They used the Internet for research, shopping, and sending messages. They played games online and set up Web sites.

The Internet also made "cloud computing" available. At first, cloud computing was used for e-mail and to store data online. Later it included using online software and applications.

With the Internet, people could reach wider audiences. To publish in print media, a writer has to get past a "gatekeeper," someone who chooses what's printed. Web sites now allow people to skip the "gatekeepers" and instantly communicate with broad audiences.

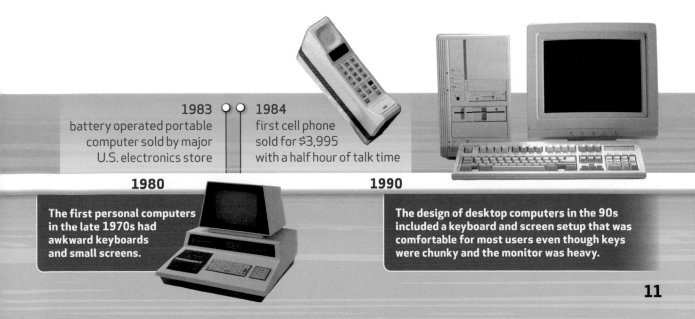

1983
battery operated portable computer sold by major U.S. electronics store

1984
first cell phone sold for $3,995 with a half hour of talk time

1980

1990

The first personal computers in the late 1970s had awkward keyboards and small screens.

The design of desktop computers in the 90s included a keyboard and screen setup that was comfortable for most users even though keys were chunky and the monitor was heavy.

From Your Hand to the World

The development of personal computers, e-mail, and the Internet in the 70s, 80s, and 90s ushered communication technology into the Millennium. Laptop computers became lighter and more powerful. The first tablet-style computer hit stores in 2002, but didn't become popular until after 2009.

At the start of the Millennium, cellular phones were the latest communication device. Life was very different before cell phones were so widely used. People could not call friends or family who were traveling or away from a phone line. People who were lost or in an accident could not call for help. Family members on the go could not easily keep in touch with one another. To call home, they needed to deposit coins in a pay phone.

Today cell phones are so small and accessible that most Americans carry them. Many homes no longer have landlines for telephone communication. Cell phones can send text messages and take pictures or videos. Newer cell phones, called smartphones, fit in your pocket, and function as a phone, a camera, and a computer with Internet access. Applications allow people to shop, watch films, hear music, do research, and keep in touch by voice or by texting.

The latest technology shifted the way users enjoyed music, read for pleasure, and socialized.

Cell phones are often used to take and send photos.

2000

2002
first cell phones with cameras

2003
Libraries begin offering free downloadable e-books.

2005

First generation e-ink reader

2004
first e-ink based e-book reading device

With the Internet, there are new ways to share opinions, news, stories, and photos. Making personal experiences public is possible with the use of blogs and social media. People can connect with friends and family any time, regardless of where they live.

From their earliest efforts at communication, people have transformed the process with their inventions. Writing systems and printing presses changed people's lives. The telegraph, telephone, radio, and television delivered messages worldwide. The Internet brought people into an age of instant communication, information, and entertainment. Nobody knows what the future holds. What's certain is that devices we use to communicate will continue to evolve, and new inventions will spring from devices we now carry in a backpack, put in our pocket, or hold in our hand.

With the onset of touch screens, tablet users can do with finger swipes what keyboards used to do.

Teens and adults communicate as much or more by short written texts. Users often decide to write rather than talk.

2011
first smart phone used on spacecraft

2010

Check In What surprised you about communication inventions from the past?

The Power of Speech

by John Manos

Unifying a Nation

Speeches have tremendous power. A good speaker can move people in a way like no other. Often it is not only the way the speaker delivers a speech that makes it historic, but also the events happening in the world at that time.

Great oration, or speaking, is not a talent of every leader. But one job of elected officials is to unify a nation in a time of a crisis. These are times when a whole nation of people needs to draw together. It is in these times that the power of a speech is at its greatest. Throughout history, many memorable speeches have been given in times of **crisis.**

A time known as *The Great Depression* had cost a quarter of Americans their jobs. People thought prosperity would never return. It was during this time that Franklin Delano Roosevelt was elected president. FDR, as he was known, delivered his **inaugural** address on March 4, 1933. It was broadcast across the country. People still quote a single phrase from the speech:

"**the only thing we have to fear is fear itself.**"

During the Depression, people stood in long lines for food. One out of every four people was without a job.

FDR combined the power of speech with an important **communication** tool of the day: the radio. Radio use was spreading, and FDR's radio speeches were known as the "Fireside Chats." Americans felt that they knew the President almost as a personal friend. FDR spoke in a way that brought safety and comfort but also encouraged. FDR asked listeners to communicate to him in response to his speeches. And people did. Millions of letters were sent and received. Roosevelt used the power of his voice and language that everyone could understand. He used stories and analogies. He helped cheer up citizens during a devastating time. And because he took special care in crafting the radio broadcasts, citizens respected him. FDR chose words that gave a sense of national identity, where everyone was on the same team, and people had hope in his words, *"Together we cannot fail."*

Roosevelt made 31 live radio speeches during his presidency.

Speeches can also unify people in times of celebration. Such speeches often focus on a shared sense of purpose. Many speeches that are given to **commemorate** an event become a rallying cry for an entire population. In 1962 at age 43, John Fitzgerald Kennedy became the youngest person ever to be elected president. He brought youthful energy to his inaugural address:

"Let the word go forth from this time and place, to friend and foe alike, that the torch has been passed to a new generation of Americans."

In his speech, Kennedy described challenges the country faced, and he called upon all to meet those challenges. At the end of the speech, he delivered a line that is often quoted:

"And so, my fellow Americans,
ask not what your country can do for you,
ask what you can do
for your country."

President Barack Obama

Speeches that unify a nation may bring us together to commemorate historic firsts. On January 20, 2009, Barack H. Obama became the first African American to be elected President of the United States. He spoke to almost two million people in Washington, D.C that day. He recalled the journey of earlier Americans, and he asked Americans to do the same:

". . . it has been the risk-takers, the doers, the makers of things . . . who have carried us up the long, rugged path towards prosperity and freedom. . . . This is the journey we continue today."

Human and Civil Rights

Some speeches mark a moment in history, as they do when a new president takes office. A great speech can also change history. This has been especially true in the struggle to achieve human and civil rights.

The "I Have a Dream" speech is considered one of the greatest civil rights' speeches in U.S. history. Martin Luther King, Jr. delivered it on August 28, 1963, when African Americans were free from slavery but still denied basic freedoms in many parts of the country. Dr. King offered a vision of hope and change. His speech helped reshape the course of our entire American society:

"I have a dream that one day this nation will rise up and live out the true meaning of its creed: 'We hold these truths to be self-evident, that all men are created equal.'

I have a dream that one day on the red hills of Georgia, the sons of former slaves and the sons of former slave owners will be able to sit down together at the table of brotherhood."

"I have a dream that my four little children will one day live in a nation where they will not be judged by the color of their skin but by the content of their character."

Mohandas Gandhi of India was one of Dr. King's heroes. Gandhi believed that the only way to achieve civil rights was through nonviolent means. On August 8, 1942, in Bombay (now Mumbai) he described his goals:

Mohandas Gandhi

"Ours is not a drive for power but purely a nonviolent fight for India's independence . . . In the democracy which I have envisaged, a democracy established by nonviolence, there will be equal freedom for all. Everybody will be his own master."

Great Feats and Broken Barriers

Sandra Day O'Connor

Accomplishments, important events, and falling barriers all lead to great speeches. We commemorate the achievements through speeches as they occur and afterward in remembrances.

In 1981, President Ronald Reagan nominated Sandra Day O'Connor as the first female Supreme Court Justice in U.S. history. In 2004, O'Connor described herself as "a cowgirl from Eastern Arizona" and explained that the nomination "...*was about women everywhere. It was about a nation that was on its way to bridging a chasm between genders that had divided us for too long.*"

Some barriers are physical as well as political. For example, the Berlin Wall was built on April 13, 1961, during a time known as *The Cold War.* On June 12, 1987, President Ronald Reagan delivered a speech in front of the main gate in the Berlin Wall. He spoke to people behind the Wall who could only hear his speech **transmitted** through illegal radio broadcasts. He called on the leader of the Soviet Union, Mikhail Gorbachev, to make a profound change announcing, *"General Secretary Gorbachev, if you seek peace, if you seek prosperity for the Soviet Union and Eastern Europe, if you seek liberalization: Come here to this gate!"*

Reagan's speech signaled the beginning of the end of communism in Europe. Two years later, the Wall came down.

"Mr. Gorbachev, open this gate! Mr. Gorbachev, tear down this wall!"

Women's Voices

Throughout history, great speeches inspired many to celebrate or act in a new way. Many of these speeches were given by men. But many were also given by women, and not only those who held political positions. Women who were common citizens made history communicating in their own style.

Sojourner Truth

Sojourner Truth was born into slavery and when she was finally free, she spoke often about the rights of all people, particularly women. In 1851, she gave an unplanned speech at a convention for women's rights. One issue of the day was whether women should be able to vote in a political election.

After a life of hard work in fields, Sojourner Truth knew she had abilities equal to men. *"Look at me! Look at my arm!"* she said. *"I have ploughed and planted, and gathered into barns, and no man could head me!"* This meant that no man could outdo her. At the time, if women were allowed to vote, there was the concern that only white women would be able to do so. Sojourner Truth wanted to communicate that all women, white and black, should have the right to vote. She added thoughtfully, *"And ain't I a woman?"*

President Obama nominated Hillary Rodham Clinton to the role of U.S. Secretary of State in 2009. Before she played this role, Clinton had been a First Lady and a U.S. Senator. One of the Secretary of State's duties is to speak to international leaders and diplomats. In so doing, the Secretary of State delivers the United States' messages and policies around the world. In the first three years as Secretary of State, Clinton traveled to over 90 countries, speaking often about the welfare of women and girls. In 2011, at a meeting focused on women, peace, and safety, Clinton said, *"Many of us have tried to show the world that women are not just victims of war; they are agents of peace."* In this speech, Clinton used her role as a diplomat to educate and inform. She has stated that women are critical to making changes that improve life for all people.

Hillary Rodham Clinton

"...when women organize in large numbers, **they galvanize opinion** **and help change the course of history.**"

Words Today & Tomorrow

The spoken word has the power to move us. Speeches can persuade, entertain, inform, and inspire. As in the past, great moments of the future will be made memorable through the words of future leaders and ordinary people who are devoted to making life better for others.

"Women must try to do things as men have tried. When they fail, their failure must be but a challenge to others."

—**Amelia Earhart,** aviator

". . . you can have a dream, you can have struggles, but you can overcome those struggles through perseverance and the right mentors in your lives and (by) making good decisions."

—**John Herrington,** astronaut

"Your work is going to fill a large part of your life, and the only way to be truly satisfied is to do what you believe is great work. And the only way to do great work is to love what you do."

—**Steve Jobs,** technology developer

"If you get, give. If you learn, teach."

—**Maya Angelou,** poet

"Life is not a spectator sport. . . . If you're going to spend your whole life in the grandstand just watching what goes on, in my opinion you're wasting your life."

—**Jackie Robinson,** baseball player and civil rights activist

Check In For what reasons have speeches been made throughout history?

How to Plan a Presentation
by James Weber

So you need to prepare a presentation for your classmates or a group of family members? Here's a guide to doing just that and doing it well! Speaking to an audience makes nearly everyone nervous. Choosing a topic you love, preparing with great research and a few visuals, and practicing your delivery will ensure success. You might even be able to persuade, inform, entertain, and demonstrate all in one presentation. Clear **communication** is part of many jobs and many careers require some degree of public speaking. Getting comfortable speaking in front of audiences now is a great way to prepare for your future.

The word hieroglyph comes from two Greek words that mean *sacred* and *translations*. The earliest hieroglyphic inscription may have been written around 3400 B.C. In the 4th century A.D., a Roman emperor closed all Egyptian temples where many inscriptions could be read. The meanings of hieroglyphics were not deciphered again until the early 19th century.

You can ask your audience to try and write a message in hieroglyphics.

1 Choose Your Topic

If your presentation is an assignment, you may have to meet certain criteria. However, building a presentation on a topic that interests you or one that you know a lot about is the best way to go. Here's an example: *Coded messages throughout history.* Your presentation could use the broader topic of codes to tell about ancient communication that used a code, such as hieroglyphics. You might describe Morse code, nautical flags, and other current communication codes. You could narrow your topic to make it more specific. A well-focused topic helps you with your research and your notes.

U. S. Marine Navajo Code Talkers devised an unbreakable code. They developed a code of 411 military terms. The code included a full alphabet. For example, the Navajo word for *ice* is *tkin* and in the code it stood for the letter *I*. In 2001, all living Navajo Code Talkers received Congressional Medals of Honor for their work.

2 Plan and Research

You'll need to build your presentation with research. Great research will help you **articulate** the most interesting information. Focus on your topic and purpose, and search for interesting details that will entertain and educate your audience.

For example, your listeners may not know that American Navajo Indians were "code talkers" during World War II. You can explain code talking and tell when it was useful. Or you could demonstrate a series of Morse code exchanges. You might even persuade your audience that today's use of text messages is a form of code talking.

Even though you'll be speaking for your presentation, you need to do some writing to prepare. You'll need to find the best order, or flow, for your information. So if your presentation is historical, a good choice is to order your information chronologically.

Begin with ancient codes and work your way to the present. Also, think about how to engage your audience. What will get your listeners' attention? You may want to start with an example, such as an interesting code from history. Or you could play a sample of Morse code beeps or a recording

You can create a code with a code dial. Substitute one letter of the alphabet for another. Spell out the new word. See if audience members can crack the code.

of Navajo code talkers. Then you'll need to find a way to move back to the chronological flow.

Write speaking notes and edit, just like you would for a written paper. Use your research to find information you will present. Type up pieces of information or use note cards that you can hold during the presentation. Go over your final notes and cut out details that aren't the most important, and plan a catchy ending for your presentation.

Think about your materials and visuals. Will your audience want to participate? If so, supply pens and paper so they can try to write or break a code. Would a clear visual help you launch your presentation? Design something that is easy to use. Watch out for visuals that are hard to display. Make copies of any handouts ahead of time and test out all links to Web sites.

These flags are used as an international naval alphabet. Like other coded alphabets, each flag stands for a term. Sometimes the same flag stands for a letter. For instance, the blue and yellow striped flag stands for *Golf*. This term means "I require a pilot." It also stands for the letter G.

3 Practice

Gather all of your materials, including your notes. Now use your voice. Practice reading through your notes, and speak loudly and clearly, just as you will for the presentation. Practice difficult pronunciations. As you practice, demonstrate emotion and interest by using non-verbal communication. Gestures and facial expressions can show information and enthusiasm.

Remember the purpose of your speech and choose your tone. For example, if you want to inform or demonstrate, be serious and informational. If you are comfortable adding humor, use a lighter tone.

No matter what, be yourself and your audience will appreciate it. Being sincere and showing interest in the topic are powerful tools of persuasion.

Ask a friend or family member to watch you practice and have him or her point out distracting gestures such as fidgeting. You can also practice before a mirror or, if possible, record yourself.

Now you can launch your career as a presenter! Whatever your topic, you can plan and deliver a winning presentation when you follow these steps to good public speaking.

Bring supplies for your listeners to make a nautical flag. Share the meanings of the colors and stripes. See if the group can read their meanings.

Helpful Tips

Relax. Take a deep breath to calm your nerves.

Smile. Before you begin your speech, smile and acknowledge your audience. This will **transmit** a warm, welcoming mood.

Project Your Voice. Speak slowly and clearly. Start off with a greeting, "good morning," "good afternoon," or even "hello."

Make Eye Contact. Calmly look around the whole room. As you speak, look directly at individual listeners for a few seconds.

Be confident. If you behave as if you are speaking from a position of authority, you will remain in control and be an effective presenter.

Check In   Why is it important to plan a presentation?

Discuss | Ideas

1. What connections can you make among the three pieces in *Speak Out*? How are the pieces related?

2. "Getting the Word Out" and "The Power of Speech" both present historical information. How did the writers of each selection organize the texts? What is alike and different about each text?

3. Use information from "Getting the Word Out" to share ways that communication devices changed over time. What changes do you think will happen in the future?

4. Look at the colorful quotations placed throughout "The Power of Speech." Choose one or two you like the most. What is it about the quote that appealed to you?

5. In "How To Plan a Presentation" the writer suggests activities related to codes that the audience could try. Which would you like to try and why?

6. What questions do you have about communication devices throughout history? What do you still want to learn more about?